Skydiving

SKYDIVING

←A FIRST BOOK→

by Eleanor Kay

illustrated with photographs

Franklin Watts, Inc.
845 Third Avenue
New York, N.Y. 10022

To Joe Crane

whose integrity, strength of character, and genuine interest in all kinds of people have left a legacy to those who knew him.

THE AUTHOR AND PUBLISHERS WISH TO ACKNOWLEDGE THE ASSIST-ANCE OF JAMES F. CURTIS III, ASSISTANT DIRECTOR, UNITED STATES PARACHUTE ASSOCIATION.

Cover photograph courtesy *Golden Knights*

Contents

CHAPTER 1   Out You Go!   1

CHAPTER 2   Parachuting — the Beginnings   5

CHAPTER 3   The Parachute Today   10

CHAPTER 4   Training to Jump   17

CHAPTER 5   Training the Skydiver   26

CHAPTER 6   Sport Parachuting Competitions   36

CHAPTER 7   Military Parachutists   43

CHAPTER 8   The Hazards of Skydiving   50

CHAPTER 9   Skydivers — and Why   56

Skydiving Clubs   60

Glossary of Skydiving Terms   63

Index   65

CHAPTER 1

Out You Go!

The plane was cleared for takeoff at 1:10 P.M. The pilot signaled to his passengers and pushed the throttle forward. In a few moments, the runway was left behind as the small craft pointed its nose into the sky.

The day was perfect. Small puffs of cumulus clouds dotted the sky at 18,000 feet, like fluffy balls of cotton. The temperature was in the mid-80's, with a southeasterly wind of five knots. It was just the right weather for flying, and for skydiving.

The plane's passengers — two men and a woman — had been prepared for takeoff long before the pilot had signaled. Their parachute packs were fastened securely to back and chest. They were ready to skydive.

Leveling off at 13,000 feet, the pilot again signaled to one of the skydivers. Because the door of the plane had been removed, the noise inside the cabin made talking somewhat difficult.

Pointing with his index finger in a downward gesture, the pilot

Clearing the doorway. (JERRY IRWIN)

indicated that he was making a pass over the drop area. The jumpers nodded. Then one of the men positioned himself in the open doorway.

At about 2,500 feet, a WDI (wind drift indicator) had been thrown from the plane. It is a roll of crepe paper with a metal rod at one end. The WDI floats to earth at about the same rate of speed as does an average man under a chute. The jumper had watched carefully to see in what direction the breeze was pushing the WDI. Then he had signaled the pilot that the best place to jump was a short distance back.

The pilot nodded and put the plane into a banking turn. The skydivers checked their pull rings, helmets, and goggles.

By holding up his right hand for a few seconds and then dropping it rapidly, the man acting as the jumpmaster gave the signal to jump.

In a moment the first jumper had leaped from the doorway, followed immediately by the second and third skydivers. The plane tilted slightly from the loss of weight, then straightened itself and flew off.

Jess Cranshaw, the first jumper, once again felt a great exhilaration as, high above the earth, he fell effortlessly through the sky. Spreading his arms and legs and arching his head backward, he assumed the stabilization position. In this way, he was able to maneuver his body freely. He looked above him and saw his friends, Marian and Tom, in similar positions close by. He waved to them and they waved back.

It was a truly magnificent feeling. Free and unencumbered, the three jumpers moved to the right or left at will, all the while falling

Free and unencumbered, this woman enjoys a few exciting moments in the sky. (JERRY IRWIN)

rapidly toward the earth. In a few moments, Jess checked his altimeter and pulled the rip cord near his chest. Marian and Tom did the same. The parachutes billowed out above them.

Looking below, Jess noted the exact position of the drop zone, clearly marked by a huge circle on the field. He pulled his steering lines to position himself correctly and drifted down to the drop zone in an even pattern of descent. A last-minute tug on the right-hand lines brought him within inches of the circle. He bent his knees, rolled gently into the fall, tumbling over and then onto his feet. Quickly he gathered in his chute.

Tom was now rapidly approaching the drop-zone circle. He maneuvered his steering lines carefully, and landed about four feet from where Jess had touched down. He rolled over and pulled in his grounded parachute.

Both men watched as Marian approached. Her descent was even and she pulled her lines neatly, grinning as she touched down in the exact center of the circle.

"You hit it right on the mark!" Jess called. "Now let's get back to the packing area. We can probably get in three or four jumps today if we move along."

CHAPTER 2

Parachuting—the Beginnings

One of the earliest mentions of umbrellalike parachutes came from China around 1300. Nearly two centuries later, Leonardo da Vinci, the great Italian artist and scientist, designed a parachute apparatus that could safely lower a man to earth. There were others who also mentioned the parachute or a similar type of device, but it was not until 1797 that an actual parachute jump took place. André Jacques Garnerin made a descent from 2,000 feet above Paris in a parachute which he designed. He suffered no injuries and is recorded as having made the first real parachute jump in history.

In the first parachute jump, and in the others that followed, the jumper actually rode in a gondola basket suspended beneath the canopy of the chute. No one used a packed parachute, as we know it today, until 1885.

Thomas Baldwin, an American, designed a packed unit that could be attached to a harness which the jumper wore. When he jumped, his weight, plus the gravitational pull on the lines in the pack, would pull open the chute, allowing the air to enter the canopy and expand it. The chute would open wide and the jumper could float down safely.

Parachutes of this type were used during World War I by pilots of balloons or small dirigibles. Airplane pilots, strangely enough,

Stunt flyer changes planes in midair, 1922. (UPI PHOTO)

were not issued chutes. When their planes were shot down, they went with them.

In the early 1900's, a man named Charlie Broderick came up with a new stunt for the traveling air shows that were touring the country. Most of the jumpers in these shows jumped from gondolas, enlivening their performances with acrobatics. Broderick developed a packed chute that was designed like a vest. Attached by harness to Broderick's body was the chute and a cable line that was also attached to the gondola. When Broderick leaped from the gondola, the crowd below was horrified to see no chute following him. Instead, it seemed as if he were falling to certain death!

Suddenly, as the cable played out, the pull opened the pack and the parachute unfolded. Broderick floated safely to the ground.

This type of packing made Broderick famous. No longer would the parachute be attached to a carrier, such as the gondola. The cable, or static-line, invention that pulled the parachute open was accepted and developed for military use.

From then on, jumps from airplanes were fairly successful with a wide variety of chutes, opening devices, and packs. Countries all over the world began to look for an even more satisfactory type of chute to be used by pilots in times of danger. Many inventors attempted to meet the demand.

In April, 1919, Leslie Irvin jumped from a plane at 1,500 feet, with a parachute device that he had designed. The chute contained 40 gores, or even pieces of material sewn together, and 40 suspension lines. It did not attach by static line to the vehicle that carried the jumper. Irvin's parachute opened by means of a ring that the jumper pulled himself, thrusting open the pack and allowing the canopy and lines to break free.

There was much controversy over the use of the static line versus the jumper-control pull ring. Only after a fatal accident to a qualified and experienced jumper, whose static line became tangled and then broke, were the experts convinced that the jumper pack was more practical and safer. This tragedy also convinced many that it was not the free fall that killed a jumper. The parachutist had

United States paratroops land on New Guinea, 1944. (UPI PHOTO)

thrashed about wildly until he hit ground, proving that it was the impact that killed him, not his rapid descent.

In time, the parachute became an integral part of all airborne transportation systems. Designs were streamlined, different materials were used, new harnesses were developed, as were methods of opening. A reserve pack was designed, to be worn with the original parachute.

By 1939 most major powers in the world had a defined and well-trained parachute force in their military setup. Germany's Adolf Hitler insisted that his personal bodyguards be trained as parachutists. The French army decided to train jumpers in behind-the-lines sabotage, but the plan failed because they did not have a timing device to open the chutes at the calculated moment. Therefore, the chutists often found themselves far from the actual drop zone. The project was abandoned.

In 1940 Winston Churchill ordered British paratroopers to be trained in a crash program to deal with the threatening Axis forces. Five thousand men were trained in an accelerated program that went on day and night, rain and shine, for thirty days.

Also in 1940, the United States went into parachute-training programs. The first group of recruits, all volunteers, went to Hightstown, New Jersey, after their initial training at Fort Benning, Georgia. The United States had the best safety record of any country in training parachutists. Out of the first 4,300 jumps, only 111 men were hospitalized, and none were fatally injured. Most of the injuries resulted from bad landings.

By 1945 the parachute was an accepted device for emergency lifesaving. It was not only used by the armed forces, but also by fire fighters, by rescue teams, and — as a crowd chiller — by barnstorming county-fair exhibitionists. But skydiving was still unknown.

CHAPTER 3

The Parachute Today

Most of us think of the parachute as a device used to save a flyer's life or to land airborne troops behind enemy lines. Actually, there are many other uses for the parachute. Fire fighters use them to land behind fire lines and begin a reverse fire against the original one. Parachutes have also been used successfully to drop food to trapped animals in snowbound valleys or mountain areas. They have been used to provide the same help to people trapped by flood or other disasters.

In more recent years, the parachute has been successfully installed aboard huge aircraft carriers. The chute becomes a brake for the jet plane slamming down on the carrier deck. Still more recently, the chute-brake has been used on automobiles, particularly racing cars, which travel at tremendous speeds. And, of course, everyone is familiar with the parachute attachment used in the space program to bring a capsule safely down on the water.

Skydivers especially know the worth of the air-filled sacks above their heads. (Sport parachuting, generally known by the popular term of skydiving, may be divided into two parts: maneuvering the chute to land as close to a landing target as possible; and the free-fall period before the chute opens, during which the jumper per-

Getting ready to jump. Note both chest and back chutes. (JERRY IRWIN)

forms aerial maneuvers. Most jumpers call themselves sport parachutists.)

There are three basic types of packs — the seat, the chest, and the back pack.

The seat pack is worn like a cushion or seat, which is how it got its name. It is rather bulky and is usually found in bucket-seat planes, such as those used in the Army or Navy.

The chest pack attaches to the body with a harness worn over the chest. The reserve chute, worn by anyone making a planned jump, is usually a chest chute, but it can also be worn on the back, above the regular back pack.

The back pack is the most common type. It can be manually operated or attached to a static line. The free-fall, or manually operated, pack is opened by the jumper at his own discretion when falling. The static-line pack is set to open by a line anchored to the plane.

Sport parachutes have these major parts: a small pilot chute; a sleeve; a main canopy; suspension lines; a chute container; and a harness.

When the rip cord or static line unlocks the pack, opening bands allow the spring-loaded pilot chute to jump out into the airstream. The force of the spring is enough to make the pilot chute burst out about three feet. (This will happen even if you are standing on the ground and open a packed chute.)

Once the pilot chute is deployed, it anchors itself in the airstream that is flowing from the jumper's body. This anchoring extends the sleeve, or bag-encased canopy, above the jumper. Then the suspension lines unfold. The suspension lines are packed in a zigzag man-

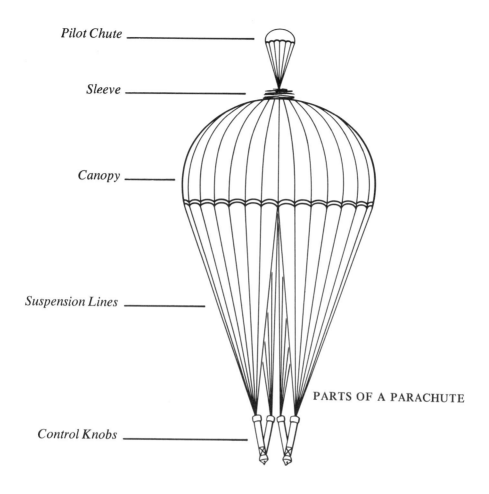

Pilot Chute _____

Sleeve _____

Canopy _____

Suspension Lines _____

PARTS OF A PARACHUTE

Control Knobs _____

ner and are secured with rubber bands. Finally, the big canopy is dragged out. All this takes three or four seconds. As the air fills the main canopy, the chute expands to its fullest dimension and the lines are stretched free to suspend it over the jumper. When a pilot chute is not used, the expansion is much faster and can give the jumper quite a jolt as the big canopy becomes filled with air.

To use a parachute safely, the jumper must understand how it is made and how he can make it work properly.

13

The canopy size used most often by sport parachutists is 28 feet in diameter. It is made of pie-shaped wedges called gores. There are 28 gores in a 28-foot chute, for instance, and 24 gores in a 24-foot chute. The gores are made of synthetic materials and are divided into panels. Each gore has four panels. They are carefully sewn together on a bias edge that helps to reinforce the stitching.

At the center of the chute is a vent. It allows air to escape from the expanded chute and prevents it from turning about rapidly due to the trapped air escaping out of the canopy's sides. The vent is about 18 inches wide, and is made in such a way that the escaping air trickles out at a determined rate so that the jumper will not lose altitude too fast or too slowly.

Normally, the number of suspension lines in a chute corresponds to the number of total gores in the canopy. Therefore, a 28-foot chute would have 28 suspension lines.

To see how a parachute works, place a bowl upside down in a bucket or sink filled with water. Pressing gently on the bowl, make it go under the water. You will see air forced out from the underneath part of the bowl on both sides — if you are pressing evenly. If you press one side harder than the other, the bowl will tilt and drop to the bottom of the water.

With a parachute, the jumper's body, extended from the harness attached to the canopy, holds the air that is escaping from the vent in the middle of the canopy. The extended parachute, open above the jumper, with air escaping gently from the vent in its center, will carry him down by the gravity pull on his own body and the proper amount of air escaping. This is much like the steady pressure on the inverted bowl, which made it go under the water.

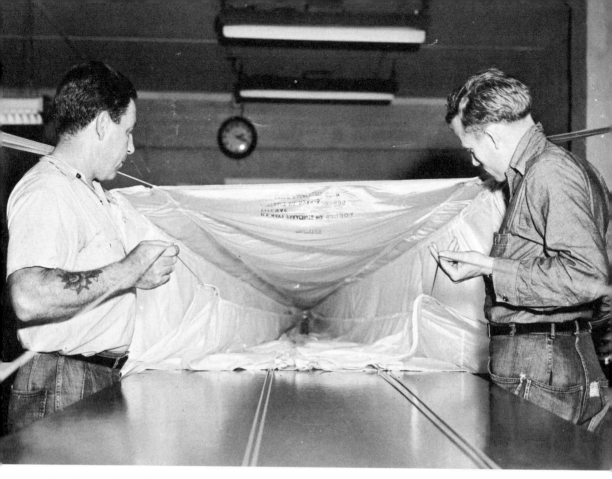

Packing a chute. (UPI PHOTO)

Although it is not a difficult job, packing a parachute requires close attention to detail. Most jumpers pack their own. However, reserve chutes must be packed by a licensed rigger, complete with his seal and signature on a packing data card. All jumpers are aware of the importance of careful packing.

Some skydiving clubs use the services of a licensed parachute rigger to pack the chutes used on a day-to-day basis. Parachute riggers qualify for their jobs by performing under expert supervision and by passing an examination.

Watching a rigger at work is a fascinating experience. He uses a long table so that the entire chute can be fully laid out. The chute is first checked carefully for damage, weak spots, or stains. If it is damp from being used in wet weather, the rigger may hang it in the drying tower. This is a tower-type room where the parachute can hang on lines that will extend it from the top of the canopy to the bottom of the suspension lines. It is not inflated. In this position, the chute will dry out thoroughly before it is laid on the table for packing.

After satisfying himself that the chute is in good condition, the rigger will begin the packing. Each gore and its panels must be folded in proper sequence. The suspension lines must be gathered and looped in proper order, and the rubber bands or nylon cords used to help the suspension lines hold their positions must be placed exactly right. Finally, the parachute must be folded properly, so that when it is pulled from the pack, it will unfold in the correct sequence, catching the air and holding the jumper aloft.

Once the chute is folded properly, it is inserted into its pack. The rip-cord is then inserted, and the chute is ready for another jump.

CHAPTER 4

Training to Jump

Unlike many sports where the participants must qualify by size, weight, or strength, in skydiving only the skill of the jumper qualifies him or her. A 100-pound person may do as well or better than a 200-pound jumper. A strong man may be beaten in points of style, accuracy, and form by a slender woman. Timing and coordination are what count in this sport.

Learning the skills and practicing them on the ground are vitally important parts of a skydiver's basic training.

As important as the physical skills is the mental attitude of the jumper. The show-off, the person who wants to be the center of attention, may as well forget about this sport. The skydiver enjoys the thrill of being in the air, being free to do whatever he wishes during his free-fall period.

Skydivers are generally average citizens who may go off after work, on weekends, or in the early morning hours for their chance in the sky. Showing off is the last thing on their minds. They understand and respect the rules of the game. They also live by them, for they know that the rules are their framework for safety. However, they may be fiercely competitive among themselves.

To become a sport parachutist, or skydiver, the student must be at least twenty-one years old, or between sixteen and twenty-one

Two men and a woman form a falling star high in the sky. (JERRY IRWIN)

with written parental consent. Because parachuting is a more expensive sport than many, there are few people who go into it for halfhearted reasons. The initial cost for equipment starts at about $200. However, most students rent their equipment from their training center.

The United States Parachute Association (originally known as the Parachute Club of America) is the national sanctioning body for sport parachuting in the United States. It is the official representative of the Fèdèration Aeronautique Internationale which sets the standards for international jumping competitions. It is also a nonprofit division of the National Aeronautic Association.

These are the USPA's minimum guidelines for parachute jumping:

1. All jumps must be recorded in a personnel logbook. This logbook must be countersigned after each jump by a licensed parachutist or pilot. (Note: Only jumps logged and signed for or legally certified will be accepted as evidence for issuance of licenses by the USPA.)

2. Civilian parachutists and student parachutists must be twenty-one years of age, or between sixteen and twenty-one years of age with written parental consent.

3. A student parachutist must pull a dummy rip cord on at least three static-line jumps under the supervision of a licensed parachutist holding at least an Orange Class B license.

4. Student parachutists must make at least five jumps in a four-place or larger aircraft with a licensed parachutist aboard, holding at least a Class C license with jumpmaster rating.

5. Each parachutist and student must be equipped as follows:

There are a number of skydiving groups all over the country. (MRS. JOSEPH CRANE)

two airworthy parachutes on a single harness consisting of a back pack with a 28-foot canopy and a chest pack with at least a 24-foot canopy. Back pack should be packed in deployment sleeve. Parachutes must meet minimum Federal safety standards as set forth in the rules of the National Aeronautic Association manual TSO C-23 and must be stamped accordingly. (Note: USPA sets no rules on the age or number of jumps limit on a parachute. Strength and porosity tests are recommended every one hundred jumps or every seven years.)

    6. Minimum opening altitude standard:

        Student parachutists   2,800 feet

7. No wings, cloth extensions, or other forms of control surfaces may be used without written authorization from USPA.

8. Student parachutists and all license holders may pack parachutes for international jumps provided that the parachutes are packed in strict accordance with the applicable directions of the manufacturer.

9. All persons engaging in parachuting shall be familiar with these regulations and with the table of rate of descent in free fall.

10. All drop-zone areas used for parachuting shall be unobstructed within the following minimum distance from the target to the nearest hazard:

Student Parachutists   300 yards

Waivers from this requirement must be obtained in writing from the USPA. (Note: A bush or tree less than thirty feet high is not classified as a hazard for legal and insurance purposes. Ditches, houses, telephone and power lines, and highways are classified as hazards.)

It is impressed upon the student parachutist that the rules were created for his safety. Abiding by them often makes the difference between parachuting with all of its thrills and pleasures and parachuting with all of the elements of danger that can be present if the parachutist is careless and uninformed.

Once the student has become thoroughly familiar with the rules, his actual training can begin. Good ground training gives the student the ability to develop the physical skills and mental attitude to become a successful skydiver. A student learns how his parachute is constructed, what it is capable of doing, and how it functions.

Every student at some time is concerned with whether or not his parachute will open. This will remain his prime concern for a number of jumps. But he learns that his equipment is dependable, and he treats it with respect. Proper care, proper handling, and proper storage of the chute are all part of his basic ground training.

Maintaining his body, exercising the control needed during the free-fall period, and gaining accuracy in striking the target zone are other prime concerns of the new student.

He will also practice many of the following steps while still "grounded" — preparing for that eagerly awaited day of the first jump.

It may seem odd, but there is a special way to move forward toward the open doorway of an airplane. The noise of rushing wind and the anticipation of the jump may make the student nervous. In order to prepare him for that, a mock-door training is used. The student learns to move forward without losing balance. He learns to keep the static line in the proper position as he moves toward the exit area.

When he has reached the door, the student now must learn the correct position. His hands, free of the static line, must be on the strut, his feet on the step. His knees are slightly bent, his head straight up, eyes looking ahead.

On the command "Go!" the jumper exits from the plane. Straight-

Static line can be seen upper right as a student experiences his first jump. (JERRY IRWIN)

ening both legs to spring up approximately six inches and out about three feet, he clears the doorway easily and immediately arches his body. His arms are spread. After the proper count, he brings his arms in to pull the rip cord, and then goes back again into a spread to maintain stability. (This is to simulate a jump when he will actually pull the rip cord. In his first jump, the static line will open the chute.)

His body is now arched enough to allow him to look at the plane above him. When he leaps out of the doorway in simulated training, the student counts out loud, "One — two — three — four — five — six." This is a simulation of the time it actually takes for the chute to open. Once on the "ground," he stays in the position in which he landed, so that his instructor can correct any faults or errors in position.

Mock-door exits and practice time are invaluable in preparing the new jumper for the real thing.

Another simulated type of training is the landing fall platform. Here the student learns various landing positions, and how to recover quickly so that he can get on his feet to pull down his chute.

The five major points of contact on a proper landing are the balls of the feet, the calves of the legs, the thighs, the buttocks, and the push-up back muscle, called the *latissimus dorsi*. If the jumper lands with his weight evenly distributed over these areas, he will have far less chance of injuring himself. The muscles will absorb the shock of impact if properly tensed before ground contact.

Before the impact, the student must tense his muscles slightly. In order to free his knee and hip joints from the shock of impact, he bends his knees slightly, relaxing the locking action of the joints

Pulling in the chute lines.
(MRS. JOSEPH CRANE)

in both the knees and the hips. Landing, rolling with the landing jolt, and recovering his upright body position as quickly as possible, the student closes down his parachute by pulling in the lines.

Over and over, he practices moving to the exit door, exiting from the doorway, and landing in the best possible position. He is now ready, at long last, for his first real jump.

CHAPTER 5

Training the Skydiver

After the first jump, the student's fears over leaving the safety of the plane are usually gone. Now his desire to become a skydiver is really tested. The few seconds of free fall until his chute opened were almost overlooked in the excitement of his first jump. Perhaps on his second jump, he will become aware of the feeling of great quiet as he drops through the air. After a few more jumps, he may wish to try what more advanced jumpers do so gracefully — make a playground of the sky as they fall toward the earth. At this stage, he will really start to learn skydiving.

Mental attitude cannot be stressed enough for the skydiver. He must remain calm in any situation. His physical responses are of great importance, too. He must exercise to improve muscle tone, to be able physically to meet any situation.

He practices deep knee bends to build firm leg muscles. Push-ups and sit-ups develop the back, chest, and arm muscles. The stationary run — standing in one spot while moving the legs in a running pattern, lifting them high off the ground toward the chest — improves circulation and breathing.

One of the first positions the skydiver learns is the stable fall position. In it, the parachutist has full control of his body in free fall — for a few seconds or during the many seconds of complicated maneuvers in competitive skydiving. In this position the diver's head is thrown back, his eyes on the horizon. His chest is raised, his back arched, and his legs spread comfortably, with the knees slightly bent. His arms are arched almost as if he is standing at attention.

In this position, the jumper does two important things for himself. He offers resistance to the air on a much larger surface of the body than he would if he were falling as if in a dive from a diving board. His resistance acts as a natural brake and reduces his falling speed. This position also gives the diver complete confidence that his chute lines will not tangle with his body. The back parachute is the one commonly used, and the stable fall position leaves his back completely free and unencumbered as he falls chest downward.

There are other free-fall positions, too. The frog, so named because the position of the arms and legs resembles a frog, gives the jumper more freedom and relaxation than the basic stable position. Most maneuvers can be easily carried out from the frog. The delta, named for its resemblance to delta-winged aircraft, enables the jumper to move downward at maximum velocity in a head-down attitude. In a true delta position, the body is straight, the arms extended backward and arched at the shoulders, pulling upward in the air. Variations are accomplished by changing the angle of the arms. In a medium delta, the arms are at a 45-degree angle.

To maneuver in the sky while falling at a great rate of speed takes lots of practice. The diver can change direction by drooping an arm or shoulder in the direction he wishes to turn, and inclining his body the same way. But it takes a great deal of experience to

The frog position. (JERRY IRWIN)

Leaving the plane in the delta position. (JERRY IRWIN)

learn the control that is needed to turn smoothly. Many, many jumps and much practice are required before even the slightest turn is made with any sort of ease.

There are other variations, too, such as the barrel roll, the back loop, and the front loop. All of these maneuvers require perfect mobility of the arms and legs in controlled movements.

Group jumps, when two or more parachutists jump from an aircraft on the same pass over a drop zone, are called "relative work." Today most skydivers are relative workers.

Baton-passing is one of the most thrilling sights to those who watch skydivers in relative work. Two jumpers exit from the plane at about 12,500 feet, passing the baton back and forth a number of times before opening their chutes at the 2,500-foot mark. They fall free at speeds up to 180 miles an hour for approximately 60 seconds.

In some baton-passing exercises, the divers' exits may vary by as much as one to two seconds. This makes it necessary for the second man to speed up his descent, while the first jumper decreases his by spreading out, so that they "catch up" with each other. A skydiver can slow his descent from 180 to as low as 120 miles an hour by spreading out his body during the free fall.

During free fall, once the rate of fall is constant, the speed of the falling body does not accelerate or decelerate in the spread-out position. This is known as terminal speed. It is figured on an average weight of approximately 250 pounds, including packs. During the first 12 seconds of the fall, the speed of fall accelerates because the gravity pull is greater than the air resistance that the falling object encounters. After 12 seconds, the air resistance builds up to where

A seventeen-year-old jumper gets ready to pass the baton. (JERRY IRWIN)

it equals the force of gravity, and the speed then becomes constant at about 174 feet per second.

This is the chart most commonly used by skydivers to figure the rate of descent.

SECONDS	FEET FALLEN	TOTAL DISTANCE EACH SECOND IN FEET
1	16	16
2	46	62
3	76	138
4	104	242
5	124	366
6	138	504
7	148	652
8	156	808
9	163	901
10	167	1,138
11	171	1,309
12	174	1,483

For each second after the 12-second mark, add 174 feet per second.

Jumpers rely on an altimeter and their eyes to determine actual altitude.

Basically, a parachute is like a big umbrella. When the rip cord is pulled, the pilot chute emerges from the pack, fills with air, and pulls out the main canopy.

"Jump" plane. (MRS. JOSEPH CRANE)

There are other factors for the would-be skydiver to consider. The amount of time a relatively new diver will be in the air, on his own, is about a two-and-one-half to three-minute canopy ride. The amount of time it takes him to get to that point may be 30 minutes or more, although the average time is generally about 8 minutes. He has to board the plane, taxi, take off, reach the proper drop-zone area, and drop the wind indicator. (The WDI is thrown on the first lift of the day. If there is no great change in wind direction or velocity, it is the only WDI thrown all day.) Over the drop area, he finally jumps. So, actual jumping takes time.

As the parachutist perfects his skill, he takes certain tests that qualify him for advanced status. A specified number of jumps, accomplishing certain free-fall periods in proper positions, hitting target areas with specified distances, and other tests will eventually qualify the jumper for a more advanced license as a parachutist.

USPA Qualifying Regulations

To qualify for Class A License

1. 25 free falls must be made, including the following:

> 12 stable delays of at least 10 seconds
> 6 stable delays of at least 20 seconds
> 3 stable delays of at least 30 seconds

2. Demonstrated ability to hold position in free fall without spinning.

3. Demonstrated ability to land within 50 meters of the center of a target on 10 free-fall jumps.

To qualify for Class B License

1. 50 free falls must be made, including the following:

> 15 stable delays of at least 30 seconds, 2 of 45 seconds

2. Complete two alternate 360-degree turns to right and left in free fall in 7 seconds or less.

3. Land within 30 yards of center of target on 15 jumps with delays of 20 seconds or longer.

To qualify for Class C License
1. 100 free falls must be made, including the following:

    100 stable delays of at least 20 seconds

    30 stable delays of at least 30 seconds

    5 stable delays of at least 45 seconds

2. Complete two alternate turns of 360 degrees to left and right within 6 seconds or less of free fall; do a left barrel loop and a right barrel loop turn.

3. Demonstrate control during free fall of vertical, horizontal, and longitudinal axis of body.

4. Land within 20 yards of the center of a target with delay of at least 30 seconds on jump, on 50 jumps.

5. Carry out a water jump.

6. Attend an instructor certification course.

7. Pass a written, oral, and practical parachute-rigging examination given by the USPA.

As you can see, the higher in skills the diver goes, the greater his range of abilities in the sky. Most competitors in international competitions hold at least Class C licenses. There is also a Class D license.

CHAPTER 6

Sport Parachuting Competitions

After World War I, a number of Americans who had been jumping as part of their military duties found that they could continue to enjoy this activity in civilian life. County fairs and air shows drew large crowds, who came to see the "crazy jumpers."

In Europe, however, sport parachuting had taken on an organized look. In France, ten government-sponsored jump areas began to produce talented and highly skilled jumpers. Other countries followed suit, and soon competitions began. In 1951 the first world parachuting championship was held in Yugoslavia. Five countries participated, not including the United States. France took top honors. In 1954 the second world championship was held in France, with the U.S.S.R. the winner. One American entered and finished twenty-first in competition with seven other countries, most of whom had entered five men each.

Although the United States was late in starting to compete in international jumping competitions, many Americans had long been interested in sport parachuting.

In 1926 Joe Crane of New York worked hard to get a scheduled parachute exhibition changed to a spot jumping contest. Crane figured that this type of demonstration would help people to understand that parachuting was not just foolish aerobatics. Finally, in

*Joe Crane gets
ready to jump, 1931.* (MRS. JOSEPH CRANE)

Crane and daughter Joyce, "mascot" of the National Parachute Jumpers Association. (MRS. JOSEPH CRANE)

1932 the first recognized American parachute competition was held at Roosevelt Field, New York City. It was called the National Air Races. Forty-six parachutists competed.

The National Aeronautic Association began to realize the worth of parachuting in the field of aviation. A parachute committee was set up, with Joe Crane at the head. Later he organized jumpers into a group known as the National Parachute Jumpers Association.

In 1956 Crane was joined by another man in his struggle to make sport parachuting accepted. Jacques Istel, along with Crane and others, began to work on a promotion plan that would fire parachuting interest in the country. Through their efforts, clubs began to be organized — in Texas, California, Massachusetts, and other states. Soon hundreds of clubs had been formed, and the Parachute Club of America (now the USPA) came into being. Joe Crane was its first president.

The United States sent a full five-man team, including Istel, to the international competition held in the U.S.S.R. in 1956. The team's equipment came largely from Istel's salesmanship ability and his contacts with interested parties who were willing to support the group. Cessna Aircraft furnished a plane, Bulova donated stopwatches, Midway Instrument Company furnished altimeters, and Pioneer Parachute Company provided the chutes. An article by Istel in *Flying Magazine* brought in some funds.

In its first full-fledged competition, the United States came in sixth out of ten countries competing.

In the 1957 meet in Yugoslavia, Istel was once again a member of the team and Joe Crane was chosen as one of the three official judges. Fifty-one jumpers competed. During the competition,

Crane, who had not jumped in twenty years, decided to try it once more. His jump into the Baltic Sea was good, but in the excitement of the event, he forgot that he couldn't swim! As a result, he had to be rescued from the water by boat. It was the 689th — and last — jump of his career. From that point on, Joe Crane was strictly an observer.

By 1960 there were over 2,000 members of the USPA. Rules were adopted that promoted safety, not only in jumping but in training student jumpers. Age limits were set, and physical examinations required. Today, the USPA, with its main headquarters in Monterey, California, has a membership of over 13,000.

Through the years, the United States parachutists increased their proficiency in the sport. They placed fourth in the 1960 competition. The 1968 world meet was held in Graz, Austria. The United States team, five men and five women, won its first world parachuting championship. The men's team finished first overall and the women's team finished second overall.

In 1970 the tenth world meet was held, once again in Bled, Yugoslavia, site of the first world competition. Donald E. Rice of the United States team became the world accuracy champion.

In world parachuting competitions, the judging of a particular event is based on a predetermined set of rules, adopted and accepted by all competitors. Five judges, using telemeters focused on the plane above them, will watch the aerial maneuvers.

There are three standard sets of international series (maneuvers) — the left, right, and cross series. The judges will watch the parachutists for execution of the required turns. They will note the smoothness with which the jumper maneuvers his body and the

Don Rice, world accuracy champion, 1970. (USPA)

amount of time taken during free-fall periods to execute the maneuver. The jumper's accuracy in hitting the target counts for points.

Each judge makes his own evaluation of the performance. The three judges then tally their scores.

Measurements of accuracy on the target zone are made by judges, who instantly pinpoint the jumper's spot of contact with a marker. The marker is then measured from the edge of the disk. Reports of the exact measurements are relayed instantly to the judges for their final computation and for noting record-breaking jumps.

As in other international sporting events, gold, silver, and bronze medals are awarded for first, second, and third places.

At the end of the day, the three winners of each event are escorted by honor guard to the platform on the jump field. The first-prize winner stands between the other two, and the national anthem of the gold-medal winner is played.

Right on the money! After leaving the plane at 3,000 feet, a jumper scores a perfect landing by striking the five-inch disc, shown beneath his foot. (JERRY IRWIN)

Largely through the efforts of Joe Crane and Jacques Istel, sport parachuting has become a recognized sport in the United States. Crane died in 1967, and many jump fields have since been named in his honor.

The United States team took first and third places at this championship meet in Orange, Massachusetts. (USPA)

CHAPTER 7

Military Parachutists

The men of the airborne forces are a unique group. Their training is rigorous and includes a great deal more time in ground training than that of the civilian trainee. It is easy to understand why. The military jumper may have to land in hills, water, or rough rocky ground, carrying 60 pounds of equipment, perhaps under enemy fire.

The military paratrooper begins his lessons under the guidance and leadership of men who are experts in the field. Jump-school training is a disciplined and coordinated period of education. The trainee learns to pack his chute under the watchful eye of his instructors. He learns to attach his harness correctly and to lace his boots properly. He also learns how to move about in the large transport planes used to drop many jumpers almost at once. In practice, he begins his jumps from a four-foot wall, working up to a twelve-foot wall, and then to a mock tower. The tower is thirty feet high and gives the student the feel of jumping from a considerable height. Dressed in full pack, the trainee goes to the top of the tower, where his harness is attached to a pulley system. At the command "Go!" he leaps from the tower. He swings through the air, and then down the pulley to the ground. As he touches ground, he assumes the proper position for contact. He must recover his position and get out of the area in a designated number of seconds.

After completing their basic ground training, the military jumpers are ready for their first leap from a transport plane. They spill from the plane at timed intervals, filling the sky with their umbrellalike chutes.

Army and Navy skydivers have formed two elite fraternities. Over the years they have grown into highly specialized and talented groups that perform at national and international competitions.

The members of the Navy parachute team are called Chuting Stars. In one sixty-day period, the fifteen-member team made a total of 1,171 practice jumps, including 162 successful baton passes and 585 free falls of one minute each. Altogether, these men logged fifteen hours of delayed free-fall time in a two-month period. The total injuries sustained by the group were two sprained ankles and one bruised heel.

The Army team, known as the Golden Knights, also has a significant record. They have performed all over the world, as well as in the United States.

In 1967 the Golden Knights set out to break all the records held by teams from other countries. These records are kept by the Fèdèration Aeronautique Internationale in France.

There were many problems connected with this all-out assault. Stacking, which means that each man leaving the plane in rotation should have a clear-enough view and a good chance at the jump sight, necessitates that each jumper have at least 50 to 75 feet between him and the man below. This is difficult to plan. The Golden Knights planned so well that each one of the three-man team hit the

Golden Knights prepare for an exhibition. (GOLDEN KNIGHT PHOTO)

Golden Knights in a tight diamond formation. (GOLDEN KNIGHT PHOTO)

target center. They jumped from 600 meters, or 1,969 feet above the ground, onto a six-inch disc.

The Golden Knights were the first team with this perfect score.

There were many other jumps on that particular day and in the days following. A nine-man team broke the previous record for 600-meter jumps with delay, meaning a free-fall period before the opening of the chute, and then landing as close to the center of the target as possible. The record had been 2.00 meters from the center. The Army team set a record of 1.58 meters.

In the individual jump of 600 meters without delay, an Army sergeant hit the target dead center on his two jumps, taking the world's record. A chutist must make two jumps within twelve hours, and the average between the two is his score. The sergeant was perfect on both.

During this competition, the Golden Knights recorded 64 new world records, including two held by American civilian jumpers and six the Golden Knights had held themselves. They made a total of 837 jumps on 108 individual and team attempts. Each man usually jumped more than fifteen times a day.

The Golden Knights use special equipment in jumping. Each team member wears black and gold coveralls which zip over his regular Army uniform. His paraboots are made with a double thickness of leather at the ankle, and the sole is filled with air pockets to help absorb the impact on landing. His helmet is gold, with the word "Army" printed on it.

The parachute used by the team is known as the Paracommander. It has 36 additional gores on the 24-foot canopy, permitting a high degree of control and maneuverability. In addition, the men use

reserve chutes with 24-foot canopies. The reserve chute has been used in about one out of 100,000 jumps.

Although each member of the military airborne forces is well trained and well qualified, not every Army jumper can become part of the Golden Knights. These are the qualifications, according to the United States Army Paratroopers Manual:

1. Applicant must be a member of the Regular Army or sign a statement of intent to reenlist.

2. Applicant must volunteer for duty within the parachute team.

3. Applicant must be a qualified military parachutist.

4. Applicant must hold a Class D international parachutist license (which includes 205 free-fall jumps).

5. Applicant must have no conviction by a military court.

The Army team includes four officers and forty-two enlisted men. There is also an aviation group that consists of two aircraft and their crews. The entire team is divided into two groups, for purposes of flexibility in demonstrations. A "Gold" team and a "Black" team each consist of nine parachutists, a ground-control specialist, a photographer, and a narrator.

The Golden Knights often give demonstrations of their great abilities in the air. It is an experience not to be missed.

The Paracommander gives the skydiver good control and maneuverability. (GOLDEN KNIGHT PHOTO)

49

CHAPTER 8

The Hazards of Skydiving

Like any other sport, skydiving has hazards as well as rewards. But the use of proper equipment and strict adherence to the rules can minimize the dangers. In skydiving, the dangers are also reduced by careful planning and good training.

Equipment failure is a potential danger, as it is in many sports. In parachuting, the jumper always makes sure that he has a back-up chute. No skydiver takes to the air with just one chute.

Landing on a bad surface can cause injury. Skydivers can usually avoid this hazard by the wind projection test and by using a proper jump zone. If wind gusts occur, the jumper may have to do some quick maneuvering to get himself back on course. Sometimes this cannot be done, and the jumper may have to land in an area of trees, water, rocks, or even houses. Careful maneuvering of the guidelines and good body position can help to minimize injuries.

With experienced skydivers, jumps from high altitudes may cause oxygen thinness. At 15,000 feet some divers, before jumping, have

A skydiver always wears a back-up chute. (JERRY IRWIN)

These divers perform a difficult feat with a hoop. (JERRY IRWIN)

found that reaction time and judgment were slightly impaired, even though they were not aware of any feeling of breathlessness. This can happen in an airplane that does not carry supplemental oxygen supplies. Naturally, the diver exiting from the plane in this condition may suffer more serious problems if he attempts a free fall from that altitude. USPA regulations say that jumps may be made from 15,000 feet provided that the time spent above 8,000 feet before leaving the plane does not exceed 30 minutes. This helps to ensure that oxygen thinness will not be a factor.

Temperature changes or extreme variations in weather conditions often may produce difficult conditions for the skydiver. At high altitudes the temperature is considerably lower than that on the ground. Helmets, goggles, and gloves are a must for high-altitude jumping. Very few sport parachutists go without them.

Mid-air collisions are actually not common but can be very dangerous. In situations where jumpers work together in the sky, as in baton-passing, both divers open their chutes within a relatively short distance from one another. If the chutes were to collide, one might collapse, causing the jumper to fall to the ground. Swift and skillful maneuvering of the chute lines makes the difference between collision and safety.

There are some dangers in nonscheduled jumps, as in the case of an emergency exit from a damaged aircraft. Jumping into city streets, highways, or railroad tracks can often result in injuries to the jumper and others. However, the danger is less than crashing in the plane.

Wind velocity can often greatly affect the ability of the jumper to make a safe landing. Once on the ground he must collapse his parachute and pull it in. The jumper who does not do so may be unable to regain his proper body position and can be dragged by the half-collapsed chute.

In the air the jumper must reckon with the wind factor that may alter his original jump target. Sudden gusts of wind may take him off course. Maneuvering his lines will help. The jumper's ability to adjust to the new situation and to seek out an alternative landing

site quickly may make all the difference between safety and injury.

A chute may open unintentionally, although this is rare. It mostly happens when the rip-cord handle snags on some object. The jumper may then be dragged from the plane unprepared for the actual jump.

Strangely, many casualties in skydiving or parachuting occur simply because the jumper does not pull the rip cord. There is no explanation for this. Some feel that a jumper may become disoriented and be unaware of his position above the ground. He becomes, it is said, totally involved in his performance and shifts his emphasis from chute opening, which should be his main concern, to free fall. Understandably, this preoccupation can prove fatal.

It is true that there are hazards in skydiving. But when the rules are strictly followed, the dangers are greatly reduced.

One after the other, skydivers
clear the aircraft. (JERRY IRWIN)

CHAPTER 9

Skydivers — and Why

You are in an airplane about 14,000 feet above the ground. All you can see from the window are miles of blue sky and hazy white swirls of clouds. The pilot announces that he is leveling off at 15,000 feet. Now you can see big puffs of billowing clouds here and there. Below, the ground looks green and brown, dotted with the shining blue reflections of water.

The jumpmaster gives you a signal, and you shuffle toward the doorway of the plane. At his next signal, you leap into the blue sky.

You turn your body slightly to look at the plane moving slowly away from you. Now you feel truly alone in the sky. There is no noise, just a gentle swishing in your ears. There is no sensation of falling — yet, of course, you know that you are. You turn around once more and glimpse the sun glistening on a lake far below.

After a 75-second delayed fall, you pull the rip cord. The pilot chute spurts out, immediately followed by the big billowing canopy. As you feel the pull of the chute, you are once again aware of being

56

Out you go! (JERRY IRWIN)

Skydiver leaps headfirst out of the aircraft, as photographer (hand in fore-ground) starts the camera. (JERRY IRWIN)

attached to earth. And now you float gently and peacefully to the ground. You have experienced the unique feeling of being a skydiver.

Who are these people that look forward to these few moments in the sky?

The participants are often business or professional people, as well as college students and members of the military. Some civilians jump on weekends at small private airports all over the country. They jump because they love to.

No one takes up skydiving in a reckless way. Jumpers have a healthy respect for the inherent dangers and they act accordingly. One aim of sport parachuting is accuracy — to head for, and come as close as possible to, a predetermined target. Another aim of skydiving is to maneuver the body skillfully and to move gracefully through space.

Skydiving Clubs

Perhaps you would like to watch skydivers in action. Most states have one or more USPA affiliated clubs, in the following locations:

ALABAMA: Elberta, Ft. Rucker, Huntsville, Mobile
ALASKA: Fairbanks
ARIZONA: Phoenix
ARKANSAS: Fayetteville
CALIFORNIA: Antioch, Calistoga, El Cajon, El Centro, Ft. Ord, Glendale, Livermore, Oceanside, Paramount, San Diego
COLORADO: Denver, Ft. Collins, U.S. Air Force Academy
CONNECTICUT: Ellington, Manchester
DELAWARE: Newark
DISTRICT OF COLUMBIA: Que St. SW, Washington, D.C.
FLORIDA: Cocoa Beach, Deland, Elgin AFB, Ft. Lauderdale, Ft. Walton Beach, Gainesville, Indiantown, Kissimmee, MacDill AFB, Sarasota, Tampa
GEORGIA: Atlanta, Ft. Benning, Hinesville
HAWAII: Monte Fields, Oahu
IDAHO: Blackfoot, Boise
ILLINOIS: Carbondale, Champaign, Greenville, Joliet, Normal, Sterling

INDIANA: Gary, Holland, Indianapolis

IOWA: Ames, Marion

KANSAS: Leavenworth, Manhattan

KENTUCKY: Ft. Campbell, Louisville

LOUISIANA: England AFB, Hammond, New Orleans

MAINE: Millinocket

MARYLAND: College Park, Patuxent River, Ridgeley, Williamsport

MASSACHUSETTS: Amherst, Ft. Devens, Orange, Pepperell

MICHIGAN: Kalamazoo

MINNESOTA: Minneapolis, St. Paul

MISSISSIPPI: No USPA affiliated clubs. General aviation district office located in Jackson.

MISSOURI: No USPA affiliated clubs. General aviation district office located in Berkeley.

MONTANA: Kalispell

NEBRASKA: Lincoln, Omaha

NEVADA: Las Vegas, Reno, Sparks

NEW HAMPSHIRE: Rochester

NEW JERSEY: Burlington, Lakehurst, Lakewood, Matawan

NEW MEXICO: Albuquerque

NEW YORK: Camillus, Nyack, Patchogue, Sh-wan-ga, West Point

NORTH CAROLINA: Charlotte, Cherry Point, Ft. Bragg

NORTH DAKOTA: Fargo, Grand Forks

OHIO: Centerville, Fairborn, Oregon, Salem

OKLAHOMA: Ft. Sill, Oklahoma City, Stillwater

OREGON: Medford, Portland

PENNSYLVANIA: Elizabethtown, Lewisburg, New Hanover, Pittsburgh, Williamsport, York

61

RHODE ISLAND: No USPA affiliated clubs. Drop zone located at Richmond Airpark.

SOUTH CAROLINA: Clemson, Hanahan

SOUTH DAKOTA: Sioux Falls

TENNESSEE: Covington, Nashville

TEXAS: Abilene, Amarillo, Dallas, Ft. Sam Houston, Ft. Worth, Houston, Lubbock, Nederland

UTAH: No USPA affiliated clubs. General aviation district office located in Salt Lake City.

VERMONT: No USPA affiliated clubs.

VIRGINIA: Arlington, Ft. Myer, Richmond, Suffolk

WASHINGTON: Kennewick, Moses Lake, Snohomish, Spokane

WEST VIRGINIA: No USPA affiliated clubs. General aviation district office located in Charleston.

WISCONSIN: Hales Corners, Lone Rock, Madison, Milwaukee, Osceola, Reeseville

WYOMING: No USPA affiliated clubs. General aviation district office located in Cheyenne.

Glossary of Skydiving Terms

CANOPY: Portion of parachute consisting of fabric and suspension lines.

CHUTING STARS: United States Navy parachute team.

CONTAINER: Holds canopy.

DEPLOYMENT: Operation of parachute from the time it plays out of its container until it inflates with air.

DRIFT: Horizontal displacement of a descending parachute.

DROP ZONE: Area in which parachutists are supposed to land.

FLOTATION GEAR: Equipment worn by jumpers who are planning a jump near water; primarily concerned with keeping the jumper above water.

FROG POSITION: Basic skydiving position, resembling crouching frog, which gives great maneuverability during free fall.

GOLDEN KNIGHTS: United States Army parachuting team.

GORE: Pie-shaped pieces of cloth sewn together to make total canopy.

MALFUNCTION: Complete or partial failure of the canopy to achieve proper opening within correct period of time.

PILOT CHUTE: Small parachute attached to the canopy to accelerate deployment of larger chute in an orderly sequence.

RELATIVE WORK: Two or more jumpers exiting aircraft on the same pass over a drop zone.

RESERVE CHUTE: Second parachute usually worn on chest and used in the event of malfunction of the main chute.

RIP CORD: Device used to activate the parachute when pulled.

SLOT: A vent constructed in the gore of a canopy.

STABILIZATION POSITION: Basic position assumed in free-fall period.

STATIC LINE: Line or cable, one end fastened to pack and the other to some part of the launching vehicle, used to open the pack.

SUSPENSION LINES: Cords that connect the canopy to the harness.

UNITED STATES PARACHUTE ASSOCIATION (USPA): Formerly Parachute Club of America; largest sport parachuting group and national sanctioning body in the United States.

VENT: Opening in the surface of the canopy.

Index

Aerial maneuvers, 12, 26-27, 34, 39-40
Aims of skydiving, 59
Air shows, 6-7
Airplanes used in skydiving, 1-2, 22, 56
Altimeter, 3

Baldwin, Thomas, 5
Baton-passing, 30
Broderick, Charlie, 6-7

Canopy, 12, 13, 14, 32, 56
Chest pack, 12
Chuting stars, 44
Competitions, 36-42
Costs, 19
Crane, Joe, 36-42

Delta position, 27
Drop area, 2, 3, 4, 33, 34

Equipment, 2, 47, 53
    See also Parachutes.
Exercises, 26

Fall, rate of, 30, 32
Fèdèration Aeronautique Internationale,
    19, 44
Free-fall period, 10-11, 22, 27, 30, 34, 56
Frog position, 27

Garnerin, André Jacques, 5
Golden Knights, 44-49

Gores, 14, 16
Group jumps. See Relative work.

Hazards, 50-55

Irvin, Leslie, 7
Istel, Jacques, 38-42
Jumpmaster, 2, 56

Landing, 24-25, 50
Licenses, qualifying regulations for, 34-
    35

Mental attitude, 26
Mid-air collisions, 53

National Aeronautic Assoc., 38
National Air Races, 38
National Parachute Jumpers Assoc., 38
Nonscheduled jumps, 53

Oxygen thinness, 50, 52-53

Parachute Club of America, 19, 38
Parachute clubs, 38, 60-62
Parachute packing, 15-16
Parachute riggers, 15-16
Parachutes, 1, 32, 55
    early, 5-9
    military, 9, 12, 43-49
    modern, 10-16
    Paracommander, 47, 49

safety standards, 19-21
types of, 12
uses, 10
Paratroopers, military, 43-49
Pilot chute, 12, 32
Pull ring, 7

Relative work, 30
Reserve packs, 9, 12, 15, 49
Rice, Donald E., 39
Rip cord, 12, 16, 24, 32, 55, 56

Safety standards, 19-21
Seat pack, 12
Skydiving techniques, 1-4
Sleeve, 12

Stabilization position, 2
Stable fall position, 26-27
Stacking, 44, 47
Static line, 7, 12, 24
Steering lines, 3
Suspension lines, 12-13, 14, 16

Target zone, 22, 40
Terminal speed, 30
Training, 17-25

United States Parachute Association
(USPA) 19-21, 38, 39, 52

Wind drift indicator, 2, 33, 34